The Tenement Writer

• • •

An Immigrant's Story

By Ben Sonder

Alex Haley, General Editor

Illustrations By Meryl Rosner

RSVP

RAINTREE
STECK-VAUGHN
PUBLISHERS
The Steck-Vaughn Company

Austin, Texas

To the Olshanskys and Benditsens and their future in America.

Published by Steck-Vaughn Company.

Cover art by Meryl Rosner

Printed in the United States of America
7 8 9 10 R 05 04 03 02 01 00

Library of Congress Cataloging-in-Publication Data

Sonder, Ben, 1954–
    The tenement writer: an immigrant's story/by Ben Sonder; illustrations by Meryl Rosner.
        p. cm—(Stories of America)
    Summary: Follows a young Jewish immigrant from Poland as she struggles to build a new life in America and fulfill her dreams of becoming a writer.
    ISBN 0-8114-7235-3 — ISBN 0-8114-8075-5(pbk.)
    1. Yezierska, Anzia, 1880?-1970—Biography—Juvenile literature. 2. Authors, American—20th century—Biography—Juvenile literature. 3. Jews—New York(N.Y.)—Biography—Juvenile literature. 4. Immigrants—New York(N.Y.)—Biography—Juvenile literature. 5. Lower East Side(New York, N.Y.)—Biography—Juvenile literature. 6. New York(N.Y.)—Biography—Juvenile literature. [1. Yezierska, Anzia, 1880?–1970. 2. Authors, American. 3. Jews—United States—Biography.] I.Rosner, Meryl, ill. II. Title. III. Series.
PS3547.E95Z89 1993
813'.52—dc20
[B]   92-14400
                                                                    CIP
                                                                     AC
ISBN 0-8114-7235-3
ISBN 0-8114-8075-5

Introduction
by Alex Haley, General Editor

Newcomers to America have never had it easy. There have always been hardships. The story you are about to read will make that clear. Most newcomers had to struggle to survive. They arrived poor. They lived in slums and worked at whatever jobs they could find. Some weren't lucky enough ever to find a real job, however bad, or an apartment in a slum. Some lived, worked, and died on the street.

Survival was only one part of the problem of coming to America. Another was acceptance. Many Americans resented the newcomers because they were "different," because they took jobs away from "real Americans," because they didn't understand English. Newcomers had to struggle to fit in. They spoke English poorly and with an accent. They wore clothes that combined American styles with Old World styles. They tried to fit in but were usually laughed at for their efforts. It was not easy.

Today it is the same. Newcomers arrive in the Promised Land and fight to survive and fit in. We should pay attention to our history and to the daily struggles of today's newcomers. We should remember that their experience was our experience or the experience of our parents or grandparents or great-grandparents. We should do what we can to help them.

Contents

• • •

1

...

Hunger

In the Polish village of Plotsk, a seven-year-old girl named Anzia stood at the window of her family's one-room mud hut. Her stomach gnawed with hunger.

Behind her she heard the murmur of Hebrew, the ancient religious language of the Jews. Her father, the rabbi, was chanting prayers with his students.

Anzia watched her father bending over his prayer book. His long red beard almost touched the book's pages. Each time he chanted a verse, his students, who were all boys, looked down at their books and repeated the verse carefully. Among them strutted a hen and her chicks, pecking at the mud floor.

While the rabbi sang the prayers and the boys repeated them, Anzia's mother sat in a corner of the mud hut peeling potatoes. She put the potatoes into a big iron pot to steam. Then she began to cut pieces of black bread.

Anzia could smell the potatoes cooking. The smell forced her thoughts back to food. To try to take her mind off her hunger, she grabbed the end of her thick red braid and squeezed it. She was so hungry, she almost stuck the braid into her mouth. Her blue eyes started to well with tears. When could she eat? Would it be such a crime to leave the window just for a moment?

Anzia knew her father would be furious if she left the window. He had stationed her there to warn him in case any soldiers came by. In that part of Poland, it was against the law for Jews to give religious lessons in their homes. If the soldiers caught them, her father would be fined or put into prison. And if the soldiers were in an especially bad mood, they might enjoy smashing the windows of a Jewish house or even setting it on fire.

So Anzia stayed at the window. She tried to pass the time by tracing pictures in the steam on the glass with one freckled finger. Anzia couldn't read or write, so she pretended that the pictures were letters. And she wished that she could learn to read and write like the boys who were her father's students. But learning was believed to be a boy's occupation among the Jewish villagers of Poland. Girls learned to cook. They learned to prepare the house for all the Jewish holy days. But they were never sent to school.

Suddenly the singing of prayers came to an end. And just as quickly, all the boys dropped their prayer books and rushed toward the table upon which the potatoes now sat steaming.

Anzia knew she was supposed to stay at the window until the students left. But she was afraid they would eat her share. She ran to the table and pushed through the boys. She grabbed a warm potato and took a huge bite. Just as she began to chew, she heard a loud banging.

The hut began to shake. The door was kicked open by a shiny boot. In strode a soldier, lashing a long whip through the air. The students turned pale and ran from the hut, the whip biting at their heels. Watching the frightened boys flee sent a cold smile of pleasure across the soldier's face. He glared after them. Then, turning to the rabbi, he began shouting threats. Next time, he warned, the rabbi might not be so lucky. Anzia's father trembled with anger and fear. The soldier threatened him with a year or more in jail and a fine so large that the whole village together couldn't pay it.

As the soldier stalked out of the hut, Anzia's father crumbled. He put his head in his hands and wept. These were not idle threats. The soldier could do this and worse if he wanted. The rabbi knew this. He also knew it wasn't luck or kindness that stopped the soldier this time. The soldier enjoyed his work. He would be back.

The rabbi's school was closed. How, he asked, would he ever earn a living without his school?

But there was no time to answer his question. Everyone in the village was running toward the hut. They came streaming through the door the soldier had smashed open. They began shouting and pointing at an envelope clutched in a woman's hand. It was a letter from America. And no one in the village except Anzia's father—and perhaps a couple of his students—could read well enough to tell them what the letter said.

Anzia watched her father unfold the letter. How she wished she could read! Her father began to pronounce the words out loud.

The letter was from a poor Jew from their vil-

lage. Just the year before he had left for America in search of a better life. Now he boasted about how rich he had become. According to him, there was work and money for everybody in America. Even the streets were paved with gold. There were no soldiers, either. You could do and say what you pleased.

On and on the letter went, describing America—a paradise of freedom and riches. The writer said that in America, Jews and Christians lived together in harmony. School was free, and anyone could go. Anzia's heart beat faster. Did "anyone" include girls as well?

The rabbi came to the end of the letter. Speechless with wonder and longing, the villagers left the hut. If only they could find the money for the trip to America. If only. . . .

Suddenly, with a yelp of excitement, Anzia ran to a chest to seize her most valuable possession, a bright red petticoat. She begged her parents to sell it. Her parents looked at her in astonishment. They knew the petticoat wouldn't bring much—certainly not enough for even one passage to America.

Then Anzia explained. Didn't they see the answer to her father's problem? They would sell *everything* they owned. They would go to America!

But raising enough money to pay for all of their passages to America took time. Anzia's eldest brother, Meyer, was sent on ahead. He could get things started in America for them. They would come later, but soon. And then their father would set up his school in America, and all their problems would be over.

2

...

The Promised Land

A few years later, a ship carrying Anzia, her parents, her three sisters, and her three brothers steamed into New York Harbor. It was the spring of 1890. The anxious family peered over the ship's railing, searching the crowd on the dock of the Castle Garden immigration station for the familiar face of Meyer Yeziersky. A sea of strange faces stared back at them.

Meyer must be somewhere on that dock. But where? His letter had promised that he would be there to meet the family when their ship came in. They needed his help. Before they could enter the country, the immigration officials were going to ask them a lot of complicated questions and would make them take medical exams.

Finally Anzia spotted someone who looked a little familiar across the bridge that connected the Castle Garden immigration station with Manhattan. He did look a little like her brother—but just a little. He was all dressed up in American-style clothes. Could that really be the brother she said goodbye to just a few short years before? She doubted it.

Suddenly the man began to wave at her, and at that moment she realized it really was her brother. But how strange he looked and acted! Though his family didn't know it yet, even his name had changed.

He wasn't Meyer Yeziersky, Polish immigrant, anymore, but Max Mayer, American. When he had arrived in America, the immigration officials had given him a new name. His real, strange-sounding Polish name had been too difficult for them to pronounce, so they had changed it.

Now immigration officials were herding Anzia, her family, and all the other new immigrants—the greenhorns, as they were called—off the boat and into the station. One by one, the immigrants were lined up and were examined by a doctor. If they were not found to be healthy, they could be sent back to the lands they had left behind.

After everyone in Anzia's family had been examined, Max was called to join his family. They hugged and kissed and made a fuss over each other until stopped by the impatient immigration officials.

The officials were going to ask Anzia's father some questions. They would ask in English, and Max would have to translate the questions into Yiddish for his father. Then he would translate his father's answers from Yiddish to English for the officials. There were many questions. Why had they come to America? What had they done for a living in the Old Country? What would they do here?

Anzia's family was puzzled by all of the questions. No one said anything about this in the letters from America! What would happen if the officials didn't like one of their answers? Would they be sent to jail? Would they be sent back to Poland?

Finally Max smiled at them. The questions were over. In Yiddish he told them everything was fine; they could go soon.

But first, like Max, they would all receive new names. Every member of the family received a new American-sounding name. Anzia's sister

Mascha became Annie. Another sister, named Fania, was to be called Felicia. And in the time it took to blink an eye, Anzia stopped being Anzia Yezierska and became Hattie Mayer.

Hattie and her family followed Max off the bridge leading from the immigration station and onto the streets of New York. Hattie's heart began to beat wildly.

What a noisy, dirty, crowded place this America was! Where were those golden streets everybody had talked about? All she saw was dirty pavement littered with old newspapers. There were no mud huts to live in like the ones in Plotsk. There weren't even any real houses. Just rows and rows of tall brick buildings with grimy windows and rusty fire escapes.

Max Mayer led them up a street called Broadway and under an enormous bridge of stone and steel. In all her life, Hattie had seen nothing like this giant bridge. People and carriages and trolleys crowded the busy bridge. Beneath it passed boats with ringing bells and ships with great billowing clouds of steam. Seagulls cried like children as they circled overhead.

Away from the bridge, the streets became narrower. Now the buildings seemed to box them in like mountains. Hattie saw dirty bedding hanging from windowsills and garbage cans spilling over with trash.

A jumble of noises filled Hattie's ears. She heard police whistles, peddlers' cries, children's shouts, and the clatter of horses' hooves all at once. These horses didn't look too friendly, either. Hattie bet if you tried to pet them, they'd probably kick you hard.

As Hattie's brother led the family down an even narrower street, a shiver of fear ran through her. Was that a fight going on? She looked closer at the two people who were shouting and waving their fists in each other's faces. Then she realized it was just a woman arguing with a man selling fish.

She listened closer. The woman was shouting in Yiddish, which Hattie understood. The familiar sound of Yiddish eased Hattie's fear and confusion. The woman wanted the fish for a penny cheaper, and the fish peddler was accusing her of being stingy. Well, maybe America wasn't such a strange place after all.

Hattie's family had arrived in a New York neighborhood known as the Lower East Side. Their new home would be here. They would not

be alone. The Lower East Side was already home to most of America's Eastern European Jewish immigrants.

Hattie gazed around at the signs in store windows. Some were in English but most, she noticed, were in Yiddish. Soon she passed a bakery that sold *challah*, the traditional Sabbath[1] bread of the Jews. She saw two bearded rabbis in robes climbing into a horse-drawn trolley. They looked just like the rabbis in the Old Country. A little boy wearing a *yarmulke*[2] suddenly darted in front of her. Then he ran into the street to play stickball with a friend.

The curbside was lined with a long row of pushcarts. It looked as if you could buy everything in the world from these pushcarts. Hattie passed piles of pretzels, old wool caps, barrels of pickles and herrings, chipped cups, and stacks of soap.

Through this hodgepodge of the strange and the familiar, Hattie and her family made their way to their new home. Well, it was kind of a home. The two-room apartment to which her

---

[1] day of rest and worship

[2] skullcap worn by Jewish men and boys

brother brought the family had few windows and only one view. It looked out on the brick wall of the next building. As for smells, there were all too many—the stench from the toilets in the hallway, the odor of cabbage and onions cooking, the steam and soap of clothes being washed and wrung by hand.

The larger of the two rooms was practically airless. In the center of its low ceiling, a sputtering gas jet offered a dim light. Plaster fell from the walls into a rusty iron sink. A limp clothesline was strung over the stove.

As Hattie's mother unpacked their few possessions, Hattie gazed in confusion around the room. During the trip across the ocean, her dreams of America had created glowing pictures in her mind. How could these dreams ever come true on such crowded, dirty streets or in this dark, dreary tenement?

3

...

Settling In

It took months before Hattie got used to living in their new apartment. As miserable as life in Plotsk had been, there had always been plenty of open sky and fresh air. In their new home, it was so dark, and the air smelled stale.

The smaller of the two rooms was reserved for their father and his religious books. The only time they saw their father was at mealtimes. Then he would put down his books and come into the larger room to eat the meals of carp and garlic or pea soup or gefilte fish that had been cooked for him.

In this larger room the family lived. They worked, they slept, they cooked, they ate, they played, they argued, they washed clothes, and they bathed themselves all in this one room. Beds, tables, washtubs, wooden chairs, and an iron stove were crowded together, all seeming to shove against Hattie's family for what little space there was to sit or stand.

Hattie's mother ruled this larger room. Endless work—cooking, scrubbing, sewing, tending the family—stole her days from early morning darkness to long past the children's bedtime.

Her children helped as much as they could, but almost immediately all but Hattie were sent off to work. Money seemed just as hard to come by on the Lower East Side as it had been in Plotsk.

When summer came, the temperature rocketed. The tenement became a furnace. So at night, the whole family moved outside to the fire escape that looked out on the building opposite. Or they moved up to the roof to sleep under the stars, waking from time to time to swat the flies or mosquitoes that plagued the city.

The heat of summer drove Hattie outside during the day, too. She began to explore the streets of the Lower East Side, walking up and down the jammed sidewalks. Gradually, the sounds and sights that had startled her when she arrived began to grow more familiar.

Sometimes she sat on the steps of her building under the hot sun and watched boys and men hurrying in and out of tenements under great piles of rags and clothing. They perspired and grew red in the face. Clothing manufacturing was big business on the Lower East Side in those days. Thousands of people worked at it, including her brothers and sisters.

At other times Hattie sat on the curb, watching the pushcart peddlers hawk their goods. The chickens, fish, roasted sweet potatoes, and herring they sold made her mouth water. The things the peddlers did to get attention often made her laugh. Their cries, which were in English or Yiddish, were like songs or poems or little bits of acting.

"Sweet potatoes!" one peddler would sing out to the passersby. "Sweet, sweet potatoes—sweeter than the sweetest melody!" Or another peddler would use insults: "Go ahead, *meshugenuh*[3], pass me by. Buy his *tsfoylt*[4] herring instead of mine.

---

[3]crazy person
[4]spoiled

Your stomach will pay you back for it!"

One day, as Hattie sat watching the peddlers, a street musician stopped at her corner. He placed a violin under his chin and began to play. His music sounded like a gypsy melody. Then he sang. His song was in Yiddish, and it was about money. It said that riches never really brought anyone true happiness. It said that happiness came from helping others and in upholding the laws of the Jewish religion.

The melody of the song made Hattie feel like dancing, but the beautiful, serious words set her thoughts spinning. She thought about how poor her family was. But here was a song telling her that even money couldn't buy true happiness.

When the song was finished, Hattie ran up to the singer. She asked him who had made up such a song. The singer said it had been written by a Jewish poet named Eliakum Zunser.

As the summer wore on, Hattie heard more and more songs written by Zunser being sung in the streets. She wondered how Zunser had learned to write such beautiful words for his songs. Maybe he had learned to write like that in school.

Hattie's chance to find out about what they

taught in school came the next fall. Hattie was about eleven, still a little young to work full-time in a factory like her brothers and sisters. So her mother bought her a notebook and a used pencil case. She sewed her a new dress and sent her to school.

Hattie was filled with joy and excitement as she walked into the school building. This was the America she had sold her red petticoat for! She remembered tracing those pictures in the steam on the window of the hut in Plotsk. She had pretended they were letters. Now she was going to learn how to write for real.

But the reality of school in America was different from what Hattie had imagined. Her first day in an American classroom came as a big shock. She walked in and saw the teacher standing at the blackboard and talking. She saw the children raise their hands and then answer questions. Everybody was speaking English. Hattie didn't understand a word!

To make matters worse, all the children were dressed like real Americans, while Hattie still wore the clothing of the Old Country. She felt like the village idiot in her ankle-length dress and shawl. As she listened to the strange words being spoken, a frightened voice inside her kept repeating, "You'll never know, you'll never learn. . . ."

The next few months at school were filled with moments of panic and hopelessness. When Hattie compared herself to the other children, she felt strange and incomplete.

Some of her classmates were Jews from Poland, like Hattie herself. But they had been in this country long enough to pick up American ways. The life they led seemed completely different from hers. Some had store-bought clothes and new pencil cases. Many had real toys to play with after school, and some even went to the theater on Sunday afternoons.

These "real" Americans laughed at Hattie and joined her other classmates in calling her a greenhorn. *Greenhorn!* The word for a new immigrant, someone who had just stepped off the boat. Hattie hated being a greenhorn. She hated being made fun of for her attempts to speak English in her heavy Yiddish accent.

But soon school would be little more than a bad memory for Hattie. Her father barely worked because he couldn't find students. He was discovering that America was different than Poland. In America, not many Jews could afford to let their sons spend the day studying religion. Their sons, like his sons, had to work.

Hattie's brothers and sisters weren't making enough money to support the family. So just a few months after she had started, Hattie's parents took her out of school and put her to work as well.

When the winds of winter came to the Lower East Side, Hattie tried to forget about her unhappy time in school. She spent her days doing odd jobs to help her family survive. She peddled paper bags on the street with her brother. And some mornings, when it was still dark, she searched ash cans at the curb for leftover pieces of coal. If she found enough pieces, the family had heat when they got up. Otherwise, it would be a chilly morning in the apartment.

Before long Hattie had given up all hope of getting an education. All she thought about was having enough to eat, keeping warm, and making a living for her family.

But the glimpse of another America that Hattie had seen in public school lay buried somewhere inside her. In that other America, there were children who wore nice clothes, spoke English well, and owned toys. A hunger for that other America would build up in Hattie gradually. It would become as uncontrollable as her hunger had been for those potatoes in Plotsk.

4
Working

Many years later Hattie would write a story. It was about a little girl who hated being poor.

This girl was a skinny little thing with big-time plans. When she finally managed to get her hands on a quarter, she charmed her friend, the herring peddler, into setting her up in business. The peddler had twenty-five squashed herrings left in the bottom of his barrel. He sold them all to the girl for a quarter. Then she stood on Hester Street, a busy marketing street on the Lower East Side.

"Herrings! Herrings! Two cents apiece!" she began to scream, louder than every pushcart peddler on the block. Women carrying baskets stopped to gawk at the little girl in rags shouting at the top of her lungs.

Then they started buying. And she started wrapping each herring in newspaper as fast as she could. When all the herrings were gone, she had fifty cents—a twenty-five-cent profit! Her heart pounded with joy.

Hattie may or may not have sold herrings like the little girl she wrote about. But she was just as eager to stop being poor. For the next several years, she would have time for nothing but work. And as hard as she and her family worked, they remained poor.

First she worked as a maid for relatives. This family had arrived in America at a much earlier time than Hattie's. In return for her services, they fed her and let her live with them. But after a month, she found out that they had no intention of paying her. They thought it was enough to give her a place to sleep and food to eat. Hattie didn't agree, so she left.

Hattie moved back to her family's tenement apartment and then began a series of jobs— sewing machine operator, laundress, waitress, cook. She was all of these by the time she was fifteen. And though a teenager, she worked as hard as any adult.

Each job seemed more hopeless, more exhausting than the other. She worked twelve-hour days, six days a week, at places like Cohen's Shirt Factory. How she longed for just a little time off! But her family needed the money to pay rent and buy coal and food. She had to hand over every penny.

In those times, Hattie's workday might start at five in the morning. There might be a little milk, coffee, and oatmeal at home to get her going. Then, if she had the money, she could ride the horse car along Madison Street to Bowery and walk over to Greene Street, where many of the small factories were.

These factories were called sweatshops for good reason. As soon as the workers entered, they'd strip off as many clothes as they could—jackets, sweaters, shirts. Now they were ready to face the hot, stuffy room. Like a sardine, Hattie was packed elbow to elbow with her fellow workers. The heat from the bodies, machines, and steam made the room feel like a tropical jungle.

Work was boring and tiring. Everyone did the same thing over and over again. So Hattie sat pressing shirt after shirt or sewing on button after button or attaching collar after collar. With

each finished shirt she would rise and hang it on a rack.

The scowling foreman marched back and forth, stopping to count the finished items whenever he felt like it. Each time he counted, he acted as if something was wrong—missing buttons, wrinkled sleeves, unattached collars, or not enough finished work. Steam hissed and needles glistened. Foreheads dripped sweat.

Despite the horrible conditions, workers seldom spoke out. If you didn't keep your mouth shut, you'd lose your job.

One night Hattie was sitting at her sewing machine, chewing on a sandwich of herring and onions. The sandwich was a present from her boss. It was his way of getting all the girls to work late without pay.

As Hattie swallowed dry bites of her sandwich, she listened to another girl complaining in a whisper. The girl's boyfriend was waiting for her on the corner, and she was afraid he'd find himself another girlfriend if she kept showing up late.

Suddenly, Hattie popped up and grabbed her shawl. The other girls looked at her in astonishment.

"I don't care if the shop burns down," she

heard herself blurt out. "We sell him our days, but the nights are ours."

At first, nothing happened. Then Hattie felt the boss's hand gripping the back of her neck.

"The minute they learn a word of English, they get flies in their nose and wanna be ladies," he screamed at her. "I don't want no ladies here!"

Hattie was thrown out of the shop for good. But before the week was over, she had found another job that was just as hard and paid just as poorly. There weren't many good jobs to be found on the Lower East Side, but there were plenty of bad ones.

Hattie's days and nights of endless work continued. By the time she turned sixteen, her life still stretched before her without promise. She now spoke English, which she had picked up in sweatshops, but she could barely read or write.

Every evening after work, she would lie on her little cot in her family's tenement apartment, her heart overflowing with anger about her life.

She wondered if she would always be poor. What had happened to the education she had dreamed of, those beautiful words she had wanted to learn to read and write? By now she had almost given up dreaming about them. The pure and brave words in the songs of Eliakum Zunser were a distant echo. They seemed as far in the past as the make-believe letters she'd traced on the window of the hut in Plotsk.

5
...
Escape

One night, as Hattie trudged home from work, she felt more exhausted than usual. Her feet hurt and her fingers ached. Her head felt as if it was being squeezed by a steel band.

As she neared her family's tenement, she caught a glimpse of the janitor's daughter through the basement window. The girl was hunched over a schoolbook, and her forehead was wrinkled into a scowl. Despite the girl's obvious unhappiness, Hattie watched her with envy. This girl was learning how to read and write. Quickly, Hattie's brain hatched a plan.

Hattie moved close to the window and called to the little girl, "Hey, what you learning?"

The girl looked up with annoyance. Grumbling, she explained that she was studying synonyms, which were just words about words.

"I'm crazy about words!" shouted Hattie.

Before the girl knew what had happened, Hattie had run into the basement and grabbed the book from her hand.

The words that leapt out to Hattie from the page seemed like magic symbols. The possibility of reading them all filled her with excitement and hope. Suddenly her fatigue and her headache were gone.

Hattie handed back the precious book. She took an envelope out of her pocket. Inside it were her week's wages. Every penny of this money had to go to her mother. Every penny. . . except maybe the extra fifty cents she had earned for sweeping up the shop.

Hattie reached into the envelope and took out a fifty-cent piece. She held it before the eyes of the janitor's daughter. Would she like it? All the janitor's daughter would have to do was give her ten lessons from her schoolbooks, at five cents apiece.

The girl agreed. And Hattie started learning. With the girl's help, she learned to read better.

She learned facts. She learned to write. And when she had learned everything that the janitor's daughter knew, she made a decision. Hattie decided to attend night school.

This time, she promised herself that school would be different. She wasn't a greenhorn anymore, but a young lady with plans. This time nothing would stop her.

Hattie's decision to go to night school caused an explosion of anger at home. Her father was furious. For one thing, going to school at night would keep her away from home, where she could be helping her mother with the housework. For another, school would mean less money for the family, because books and paper and pencils cost money. How dare she withhold some of her wages to pay for her own education!

According to Hattie's father, only men needed to learn. So it was perfectly all right for her brothers to go to night school, but not for her. Women had been put on this earth to raise families, to cook, and to do housework. Hattie should have been setting her sights on finding a husband, not getting an education.

The more Hattie's father complained, the more she wanted to go to school. The fact that her father denied her the very learning she cherished filled her with rage.

More and more, she began to resent the Old World ways of her family. The sight of her weary mother toiling in the kitchen while her father sat at his books all day made her feel sorry for her mother and angry at her father.

Finally, when she was about eighteen, she packed her few possessions. She moved out of her parents' apartment and into a room of her own.

6

...

On Her Own

Hattie's room was in the Clara de Hirsch Home for young working women. It had been founded by very wealthy people who wanted to give young women on their own a chance. Some of the women who lived at the Clara de Hirsch were being trained to become cooks or paid housekeepers. Others had jobs in sweatshops and paid a small amount for room and board.

Hattie's room at the Clara de Hirsch Home wasn't very big, but it was clean and quiet. At any rate, she wasn't planning on spending much time in it. During the day, she worked at one or another sweatshop job. At night, she went to school.

By the time Hattie got to school, she had usually put in a ten- or twelve-hour day. Her back ached and her eyes burned with fatigue. But despite her exhaustion, her will to learn took over her mind and her body. It pushed her on.

Sometimes her will to learn was so strong that she made a pest of herself. At night school, question after question spilled from her lips. In fact, she asked so many questions so often that the other students became annoyed. Why does she take school so seriously, they wondered. For them, lessons were not a matter of life or death.

Every time Hattie opened her mouth to ask yet another question, some of her classmates snickered or yawned with boredom. Some even laughed out loud. Once again Hattie felt like an outsider. But this time was different. This time Hattie shut out the jeers and yawns of her classmates and kept asking her questions.

Hattie worked harder at school than she had ever worked in her life. But this work wasn't like what she did in the sweatshops. It was something she wanted, not something others said she had to do.

Before a year had passed, her reading and writing had improved immensely. She had even learned how to type. During the day, at her job, she stole every stray moment to read or study.

One workday during her lunch hour, Hattie came across a poem in a newspaper for Jewish-American workers. Some of the words in the poem looked long and hard, but in order to practice her reading, she began to sound them out.

The poem was called "The Machine," and it was written by a man named Morris Rosenfeld. It told about a factory worker and his machine, and it described the machine as some kind of mechanical, heartless master. It said that workers were slaves without a voice but that their hearts still burned for freedom and control of their own lives.

The words of the poem pierced Hattie like needles. They described exactly how she felt about the sewing machines and pressing irons at which she worked. She felt as if her own words had leapt out of her and onto the page. Suddenly she knew what she wanted from all her learning. She wanted to write poems and stories like this Morris Rosenfeld. She wanted the world to know how she felt.

The next day, during her short lunch hour, Hattie ate her salami and onion sandwich as fast as she could. The other girls were chattering

about clothes and new hair styles, but Hattie wasn't listening. On her greasy lunch bag, she hurriedly scrawled down the thoughts that had been buzzing inside her head all that morning. She wrote half in English and half in Yiddish. The next day Hattie put down more of her thoughts.

Slowly, Hattie's lunch-bag notes turned into poems. She wrote poems about the streets of the Lower East Side. She wrote about the pushcart peddlers. She wrote about her anger at the sweat-shop bosses. She wrote about hunger and greed. And she wrote about her own hopes for a better life in America.

As the months went by, Hattie began to read her poems to whomever she could get to listen. She would read to the other workers in the shop, watching their faces for a sign of their reaction. She would read to the fish peddler on the corner or the butcher next door. Once she even read to a plumber who had stopped by the Clara de Hirsch Home to fix a leaky faucet.

Big deal, is what most of them said. Big deal. "A writer she wants to be, yet!" they chuckled. But a few of them pricked up their ears as if startled, and Hattie could tell they were thinking,

"Why, that's exactly how I feel!"

Finally, Hattie took her words and her endless scraps of paper elsewhere. At that time, the Lower East Side had a few special places for free learning. They were called settlement houses. Settlement houses were community centers that had been founded to help immigrants. They gave free medical exams, taught trades, and offered courses in English and other subjects. One of them even offered a course in short story writing. So Hattie signed up.

Hattie would always remember the first time she held out her bundle of papers to the writing teacher at the settlement house. Her heart beat with a mixture of hope and fear. What would he think of her story?

The teacher thumbed rapidly through the pages. Then he told her that she had not really written a story. What she had shown him had no beginning, no middle, and no end.

Hattie argued with the teacher. The story was just how she felt about her life. Wasn't her life full of confusion and pain? Did she or anybody else know where her life was going? Did anybody know how it would end? Shouldn't her story be the same?

The teacher laughed at her. As far as he was concerned, Hattie had broken all the rules for writing good short stories. He pushed her pile of papers back across his desk to her.

Hattie went home and spent weeks rewriting. When she was finished, the story seemed so strong to her that it could have been etched in stone. So she brought it back to the class. She slid her new pile of pages back across the teacher's desk. Now he had to like it.

The teacher studied the new version for several moments. Then he handed it back to her and shook his head. According to him, her story was still all mixed up. It began in the middle of things and moved backward and forward in time. It seemed to have no ending. It was too rambling. He told her to forget about that story and start something new.

With the teacher's words ringing in her ears, Hattie stormed out of the writing class. She went back to her room at the Clara de Hirsch Home and started to write all over again. In her heart, she knew she was right. She would show them!

A few nights later, there was a knock on her door. It was Mrs. Henry Ollesheimer. Mrs. Ollesheimer was the wife of a rich banker, but she spent part of her time helping to run the Clara de Hirsch Home.

For months, Mrs. Ollesheimer had noticed Hattie trudging home with a pile of books under her arms. Late at night, she sometimes saw a ray of light creeping from under Hattie's door. She was curious and wanted to know what Hattie was up to.

Hattie told Mrs. Ollesheimer all about her life. She told her about her jobs and about night school and about her family. She even told her about her dream of becoming a writer and what the teacher had said about her story.

The more Hattie spoke, the more impressed Mrs. Ollesheimer became. Hattie seemed so bright and intense. She was serious and hard-working. Mrs. Ollesheimer wanted to find a way to help this ambitious young girl.

Finally, Mrs. Ollesheimer came up with an idea to help Hattie. She went to the board of directors of the Clara de Hirsch Home and convinced them to offer Hattie a scholarship to Columbia University.

Hattie was stunned. She had only dreamed about going to this famous university where the scholars were known throughout the world. Was it true? Could she really walk among them now? All the ideas that existed would be placed at her fingertips at the great library of Columbia University. She would study poetry and philosophy, history and literature. Then she would become a great writer.

That fall, Hattie received her scholarship and entered college. But when she saw the courses being offered, her heart fell. She would get an education all right, but not in any of the subjects that interested her.

The people who had paid her tuition wanted her to become a *cooking teacher*. Instead of taking courses like poetry, philosophy, and drama, she would have to study food production and home care. As far as Hattie's benefactors were concerned, these were the proper courses for young ladies to study.

Becoming a cooking teacher wasn't at all what Hattie had in mind. But how could she complain? These people were paying for her education. She had to take what her benefactors offered.

So she studied cooking and at the same time

found time to read books on poetry and literature and the theater. She passed all her cooking courses that semester and then enrolled for more.

Hattie's benefactors were extremely proud of her. In their minds, she had come very far. But in her mind, she had barely begun. She no more wanted to be a cooking teacher than she had wanted to be a worker in a clothing factory. What she wanted to do was write. In her heart she was certain that she could. But no one had given her the chance to prove it.

In 1904, she was graduated from Columbia. She began to teach cooking in the New York City public schools. As time passed, a single question kept returning to her mind: *When would she get a chance to lead her own life?*

For years the question remained unanswered, burning a hole in Hattie's soul.

7
...
1918

Years had passed and the world had changed. It was 1918, and World War I, the largest and most terrible war anyone had ever experienced, had finally come to an end after four long years. Life returned to normal, but everything seemed different. New ideas were changing the way many Americans thought about the world around them.

On the streets of the Lower East Side, you could still hear the same cries of pushcart peddlers, see little boys wearing yarmulkes, or catch sweatshop workers carrying huge piles of garments on their backs. You could still hear Yiddish spoken. Yet something had changed here, too.

The first generation of Jewish-American

immigrant children from eastern Europe had grown up. They were more American than their parents. They were more aware of what was happening outside the Lower East Side.

Some had fought in the war in Europe and seen what life was like in Paris, Berlin, and other great cities. A few had managed to get a good education. From these few came writers, artists, politicians, organizers, actors, singers, directors. The Lower East Side was aflame with their intelligence and the creative energy of youth released from the shadows of war.

Hattie was now a beautiful woman with long auburn hair that she knotted into a simple braid. She had velvety white skin and broad, open features. In the fourteen years since her graduation from Columbia she had endured many changes.

Some of the changes had been very painful. Her mother had died from diabetes in 1910. A year later, Hattie married but her marriage had failed after the birth of her daughter in 1912. Hattie's husband gave their child to his mother to raise.

Now Hattie lived alone in her own apartment, still supporting herself by working as a cooking teacher. As a symbol of her independence, however, she had changed her name back to Anzia, which was her original, Polish-Jewish name.

Anzia thought that her original name now fit her better than her Americanized one. Three years earlier, she had written a story called "The Free Vacation House." The story was about a poor Jewish family from the Lower East Side—a family much like that of her sister Annie.

The family is invited to take a charity vacation in the mountains. But there are all kinds of humiliating rules to remind the family that the vacation is "free." The family must keep from the sight of paying vacationers. They cannot walk on the grass. They must stay in the background.

The story was both funny and sad. It was also angry. Anzia had submitted the story to a number of magazines. After many rejections, a miracle occurred! The story was accepted by a magazine called *The Forum*. Anzia was a writer! A *published* writer!

But despite this success, Anzia still had far to go. Only one other story of hers was published after "The Free Vacation House." Two stories in four years will not pay a writer's rent. Both stories were printed without causing a stir and were followed by nothing but rejection slips.

So she continued to work away at her teaching jobs. But when she wasn't teaching, she was writing. Or she was learning more and more from her new circle of friends about art, literature, politics, and the world around her.

Anzia's friends were part of the new community of young Jewish intellectuals who frequented the Lower East Side after World War I. Like Anzia, they respected words and valued the power of ideas.

Some, like her friend Minnie Shoner Zunser, were teachers. Others, like her friend Rose Pastor Stokes, were political activists, involved in the fight for better working conditions in factories and sweatshops. Both Minnie and Rose were also writers. They published articles regularly in the *Jewish Daily Forward,* a popular Yiddish-language newspaper.

After a long day of teaching or a long weekend of writing, Anzia sometimes joined her friends in one of the cafes or cheap restaurants of the Lower East Side. While they drank coffee and ate *kugel*[5], the talk often turned to writing. They

---

[5] a kind of noodle pudding

would discuss a new book or recite poems they had just learned. Or Anzia would ask her friends to listen to some pages of a new story of hers.

With her friends Anzia went to lectures on politics and women's rights at Cooper Union, a lecture hall located at the edge of the Lower East Side. She went to summer rooftop dinners in nearby Greenwich Village where socialists, radicals, writers, and union leaders argued about world events.

Anzia haunted the settlement houses, where free concerts, art exhibitions, and lectures were attended by large crowds of eager young men and women. And she went to the many Yiddish theaters where one could see a wide variety of plays, new and old.

During these years, Anzia learned more in the cafes, settlement houses, and living rooms of the Lower East Side than she had learned in school. Mostly what she learned was that somewhere in this exciting new world of ideas there *had* to be room for her writings. Conversations, books, plays—*everything* seemed a juggling act where things from the Old Country were tossed into the air with things from this new America. Why not her stories?

All during this time, Anzia's typewriter never stopped rattling. Her files swelled with more and more stories about life on the Lower East Side. Again and again the stories were rejected, but Anzia continued to write her stories at a feverish pitch.

One day Anzia had an idea. She decided that just as she had drawn on her sister for inspiration she could draw on another person who had played an important role in her life. The next story she would write would be based on her mother.

As Anzia thought about the story, her mother's wrinkled, tired face suddenly appeared in her memory. She remembered how her mother's eyes would squint down at her sewing work because the light from the gas jet was too dim. Anzia felt as if she could actually hear again her mother's heavily accented voice—sometimes complaining and sometimes rising in laughter.

Little by little, Anzia pieced together a story based on her mother. When it was finished, she called it "The Fat of the Land." She sent the story to magazines. But as had happened countless times before, the story was rejected by everyone who saw it.

That fall, Anzia enrolled in a writing course at Columbia University. There she could test her story with an audience of writers. Surely she would discover a way to make "The Fat of the Land" a success.

One evening, the teacher called Anzia to the head of the class and asked her to read her story aloud. With all eyes upon her, Anzia took a deep breath and began.

The story told what happens when an immigrant mother's children grow up and become much more American than she is. In the story, the children, who have become successful and rich, put their mother in a luxury apartment building with a doorman and a maid. But the mother doesn't feel comfortable living like a well-to-do American. She keeps trying to live as she did when she was poor on the Lower East Side.

One day, the mother prepares a special meal with her own hands. She's glad that it is the maid's day off and that she can do the work herself. She is expecting a visitor. It is a poor Jewish woman who was her neighbor when she lived on the Lower East Side.

The old friend arrives and the two women decide to eat in the kitchen rather than in the fancy dining room. Because the maid is not there to see and disapprove, they even wipe their hands on the dish towel instead of using the new linen napkins.

The mother tells her friend how vividly she remembers the days when there were no maids or other strangers in her house—only her family. And she yearns for the time when her children looked up to her and were not embarrassed when she spoke to them in Yiddish and bad English.

This was a difficult story for Anzia to write. So many immigrant children rushed to become "American," abandoning Old World ways, shedding their accents, donning American habits and ways. Anzia, too, had done this. She hated the term "greenhorn." She fought with her parents because of their Old World ways. She had been embarrassed at how they talked, and looked, and thought.

Standing in front of the class, Anzia read the old woman's words in a voice very like her mother's. And as she read, her memories of her mother rose again into her mind and her eyes filled with tears. When she came to the end of her story, the class was silent.

Then suddenly hands were waving in the air.

Everyone seemed to have something to say. None of the opinions were favorable, or even particularly helpful. The class tore her story apart.

One student wanted to know why anyone would want to write about such an unsympathetic creature. Another felt that "The Fat of the Land" wasn't even a real story, just a mishmash of unpleasant feelings and bad English. Others pointed out all the storywriting "rules" that Anzia had broken.

Hurt but unconvinced, Anzia listened to all the complaints. Reading it aloud proved to her that the story was good the way it was. Anzia defended her story and continued to go to the class, reading and fighting for her stories.

8

...

Here Was a Person

When Anzia wasn't in class, she was out peddling her stories. Receptionists at the offices of
magazine publishers were on the lookout for the
"crazy lady." Red hair spilling from her loose bun,
Anzia would rush wild-eyed into magazine offices
and demand to see an editor. Sometimes she
managed to catch an editor by the sleeve as he or
she was leaving the office. Anzia would press a
bundle of stories into the editor's arms.

Most editors were no more impressed with
Anzia's techniques for getting published than they
were with her stories. Some, however, read the
stories anyway.

Late in the fall, a letter appeared in Anzia's

mailbox. It was from the *New Republic,* one of the most respected magazines of the day. A story of Anzia's called "Soap and Water and the Immigrant" had been accepted by the magazine.

Unlike her earlier successes, this one did more than make Anzia feel good for a little while. "Soap and Water and the Immigrant" was published, read, and *noticed.*

One of the people who noticed it was the editor of the magazine *Century.* He saw something special in the way Anzia wrote—something very different from the kind of writing he saw being published. So when he received the manuscript for "The Fat of the Land," he read it eagerly. Unlike the students and teacher of the writing class, he liked it and decided to publish it.

The spring of 1919 found Anzia in an unusual position. Her stories were in demand. Suddenly editors were not only accepting old, rejected stories from the "crazy lady," but they were now asking her to write new stories for them. In the small world of the literary magazine, Anzia was a celebrity, the hottest new writer working.

Her classmates in the Columbia writing class may have been surprised when "The Fat of the Land" was published, but they must have been shocked when it was chosen Best Short Story of 1919. Not bad for a story that wasn't a "real story." Not bad for a story that broke all the rules!

In 1920 a book of Anzia's short stories was published. It received good reviews, but its sales disappointed Anzia. She remembered the peddlers, sweatshop workers, and janitors who had listened to her early poems and liked them. Now only people interested in "literature"—editors, writers, teachers—read her work. This didn't make sense, somehow. Her stories were about peddlers, sweatshop workers, janitors, immigrant mothers and daughters. Anzia wanted these people to know about her book, to read and enjoy her stories. But how, short of peddling her books on every corner, could she reach her real audience?

Suddenly Anzia knew! Weren't newspapers the next best thing to an army of street peddlers? If she could get someone like Frank Crane, one of the most popular newspaper writers in the country, to write about her book maybe people would hear about it.

One summer afternoon Anzia charged into Frank Crane's New York office. She presented him with a copy of her book but received only a puzzled look from Crane in exchange. Flustered, Anzia began to talk and talk and talk—about Poland and being Jewish, about sweatshops and overcrowded apartments, about greenhorns and the Lower East Side.

On and on she went. Crane, a very proper man and not in very good health, held his silence. Anzia thought she was making a fool of herself in front of one of the most powerful newspapermen in America. Almost in mid-sentence, she stopped. This was horrible! The poor man thinks I'm crazy! As abruptly as she entered, Anzia fled Crane's office.

Crane, however, didn't think Anzia was crazy or a fool. In his newspaper column, which appeared in over 300 newspapers around the country, he wrote, "I got a new slant on America from Anzia Yezierska."

His entire column that week was about Anzia! This, in part, is what he wrote:

> She walked into my office one day and brought the Old World with her. She had not said three words before I saw farther into the heart of Russia and Poland than I had ever been able to do by reading many heavy books.

She was Poland.

She was the whole turgid[6] stream of European immigration pouring into our home country.

It was all as different from reading and hearing lectures and studying statistics as eating an apple is from looking at a painting of apples.

She handed me her book, *Hungry Hearts*. At first I thought she might have printed it by private subscription, after the manner of the ambitious but unrecognized. But a glance at it showed me it bore the classic imprint of one of the leading publishers.

Then she told her story, told it well, in a way to rejoice the heart of a newspaper person, in a few swift words, of keen beauty, redolent[7] with individuality.

Here was a person, I said.

When Anzia opened the newspaper that August day in 1920 and saw Frank Crane's column, she was beside herself with joy. She knew

---

[6] swollen
[7] strongly flavored

that she was one of perhaps a million people who were reading his column today. All kinds of people would learn about her and her work.

And when she read the phrase "Here was a person," it filled her with pride. She was no longer Hattie the Greenhorn. She was a person, a writer, whose name was Anzia Yezierska—the very person she had always known she would be.

Epilogue

· · ·

Anzia Yezierska went on to become one of the best-known American writers of the 1920s. Her success caused a sensation. Newspapers called her the "Sweatshop Cinderella" and published articles about her "rags to riches" life. She was invited to speak at universities and literary clubs and even took a tour of Europe.

In 1920 Hollywood bought the movie rights to one of Anzia Yezierska's books. This brought her a great deal of money. She was also invited to move to Hollywood to work on scripts. But after just a few weeks in Hollywood, Anzia moved back to New York. The money, glamor, and fame made her uncomfortable. She felt she needed to be near the poor neighborhoods that had shaped her in order to keep writing.

Anzia's story is not all that typical of most Jewish immigrants who came to the Lower East Side near the turn of the century. Few became writers. Few even became successful in any career. Most lived lives like Anzia's mother and father or like her sister Annie. They spent most of their time working—working in sweatshops and living in poverty.

For most immigrants, the new lives they built were only slightly better than the ones they left behind in the Old Country. And some only escaped the tenements by returning to the Old Country.

The many who stayed struggled year after year just to get by. When success did come to immigrant families, it came slowly. Often it was the children or grandchildren who first realized the fruits of coming to America. Success like Anzia's was not typical.

But what was typical about Anzia's experiences was the bitter struggle for acceptance. Like so many others, she was caught between two very different worlds, the Old World that her parents tried to recreate in their home and the New

World outside that home. And in both worlds she faced rejection. Her parents were reluctant to accept the American in Anzia and the New World seemed all too reluctant to make any room for her or her dreams. And this is very much the immigrant experience.

Afterword

Anzia Yezierska was a storyteller first and always. Her autobiography, *Red Ribbon on a White Horse*, contains fictional touches. Her short stories and novels included many events and details of character and place that were autobiographical. In telling her story, this book has also told the stories of some of the people she knew and others that she invented in her writings. There was too much truth in her fiction not to include them.

Notes

Page 1   Plotsk, or Plinsk, or Ploch, as it is called by various biographers of Anzia Yezierska, was a small Jewish village in a part of Poland, which, at the time, belonged to the Russian Empire. The village was a *shtetl*, which is a Yiddish word for a Jewish community located in what was called the Pale of Settlement. The Pale of Settlement was composed of twenty-five provinces within the eastern European part of the Russian Empire. The Pale of Settlement was the only area of eastern Europe where Jews were allowed to live.

Page 1   Anzia's exact age and the exact years in which the early events in this story take place are not known. There were no birth records in her village. Her parents did not record the exact days or years of their children's births. Several times in her writings, and in interviews, Anzia mentioned that until she came to America she did not even know what a birthday was or that birthdays were celebrated. Books on her life give vague or conflicting years for her birth year—between 1880 and 1886. We are presuming that she was born around 1880, making her about seven or eight years old at the story's start.

Pages 3–4   Most of the information in this tale of terror comes from a story by Anzia Yezierska in her collection *Hungry Hearts.* Whether it happened precisely as she told it in that story will never be fully known. However, raids on Jewish settlements in the Pale were common. Soldiers often attacked Jewish homes without cause, robbing them of food and money and sometimes even burning them. Sometimes these raids were ordered or instigated by the government. Even when they weren't, the raids were tolerated and the raiders rarely punished.

Pages 4–6   The letter from the villager described in this scene is typical of thousands of letters sent by Jewish immigrants to relatives who remained behind. Whether you were doing well or not in America, it was customary to boast of your good fortune. This led to much exaggeration and to the legend that streets in America were actually paved with gold. Hence, the New York port through which immigrants entered this country became known as the "Golden Door."

Page 12   Sanitation in New York City, as in all cities at the turn of the century, was awful. Garbage was dumped from windows into alleys and streets. Animals of all kinds fouled the streets. Stagnant water collected in puddles and ponds, giving off oily smells and providing homes for hosts of mosquitoes.

Page 12 There were about 25,000 pushcart peddlers on New York City's Lower East Side by the turn of the century. They sold everything that can be imagined, including eyeglasses. When buying these it was up to you to find a pair that would not only fit your head but improve your eyesight.

Page 14 Religious Jews believe that a man's head must be covered at all times to show his modesty and humility in the eyes of God. This is the reason yarmulkes were worn.

Page 16 Gefilte fish is made from combinations of pike, carp, and whitefish mixed with egg, matzo meal, and onions. It is often eaten with freshly ground horseradish. Other favorites of Jewish eastern European immigrants included *kasha* (buckwheat groats); *kugel*, a noodle pudding often baked with cinnamon; *tsimis*, a bread-crumb and carrot mixture seasoned with meat gravy; *kishke*, beef intestines stuffed with bread crumbs, vegetables, and spices; and *latkes*, onion-flavored potato pancakes. The eastern European Jewish cuisine borrowed from the traditional cuisines of peasant Poland and Russia.

Page 19 In a 1969 interview, when she was almost ninety years old, Anzia Yezierska spoke of Eliakum Zunser with great admiration. She said that he was a hero among the youth of her time, comparing him to Bob Dylan, a musical hero of the 1960s and today. This incident, which pictures

Hattie listening to the songs of Eliakum Zunser, does not come from any particular biographical source on Anzia Yezierska. However, Zunser's songs and poems were very popular at the time and undoubtedly Hattie would have heard them being played in the street.

Page 27 Sweatshops were not only miserable places to work because of the heat, lack of ventilation, and overcrowding, they were dangerous as well. In 1911, just a few years after Anzia was working regularly in the various Lower East Side sweatshops, a terrible fire occurred at the Triangle Shirtwaist factory. A crowd of horrified onlookers stood on the street and watched as worker after worker leapt to her death. The fire, which claimed 146 lives, underscored the horribly dangerous conditions sweatshop workers routinely endured. It led to some reforms in the New York City fire codes and advanced the work of union organizers among sweatshop workers.

Page 47 World War I began in 1914 and ended in 1918. The United States entered the war in the war's final year, 1917–1918. While Europe was devastated by the war, with millions of people killed and thousands of miles of destroyed land, the United States suffered much less. Still, the response of the nation was disillusionment with world politics and an outburst of reckless energy that led into the Roaring Twenties.

Pages 48–49 Hattie Mayer changed her name to Anzia Levitas soon after she married Arnold Levitas. After they were divorced and she became a successful writer, she completed the change back to her original name, Anzia

Yezierska. Anzia's daughter, Louise Levitas Henriksen, was raised by her grandmother and her father with weekly visits with her mother. In 1988 Anzia's daughter wrote an affectionate biography of her mother, *Anzia Yezierska: A Writer's Life.*

Page 49 Annie was Anzia's favorite sister. During the troubled years of Anzia's marriage and her poor relationship with her father, Annie remained supportive of Anzia. In Annie, however, Anzia saw everything she had run away from. Annie had passed into adulthood without a formal education. She was married at eighteen to a husband her father chose for her. She had five children in ten years and remained poor and overworked all through these years.

What impressed Anzia about her sister was how Annie bore her many burdens with cheerful determination. Annie told wonderfully funny stories of incidents and arguments she had with neighbors, landlords, shopkeepers, and her family. Annie could mimic all the many voices and accents that were heard on the Lower East Side. When Anzia wrote she did the same thing. She used the voices of the immigrants, blending Yiddish and broken English in a mishmash of conversation.

Page 50 Miriam, or "Minnie," Shomer was one of Anzia's best friends. She was born in Russia in 1882 and was the daughter of a well-known Russian Jewish novelist and playwright. At seventeen she met a man named Charles Zunser and married him. Charles was the son of Eliakum Zunser, the Jewish poet and songwriter Anzia admired so much.

Rose Pastor had been one of the most talked about Jewish women in America in 1905. She had fallen in love with and married James Graham Phelps Stokes, a young millionaire whose Protestant family had been in America for generations. In those days, few people married out of their religion or social class. Rose's marriage to Stokes caused a sensation. Almost every newspaper in America carried articles about it. Rose became a socialist and made fiery speeches in defense of workers' rights.

Pages 62–63   The Yiddish word for "person" is *mensch*. But in Yiddish mensch has a larger meaning than its English counterpart. It also means someone with great humanity and self-respect—in other words, a real human being. To be called a person would have carried this added meaning to Anzia, enhancing her joy at Crane's article.

Ben Sonder lives on New York City's Lower East Side. He is a writer, editor, translator, and screenwriter. Mr. Sonder is also the co-author of *Osceola, Patriot and Warrior.*